Science Links

NATURE DID IT FIRST

Susan Ring

CHELSEA CLUBHOUSE

An Imprint of Chelsea House Publishers

A Haights Cross Communications Company

Philadelphia

This edition first published in 2003 by Chelsea Clubhouse, a division of
Chelsea House Publishers and a subsidiary of Haights Cross Communications.

A Haights Cross Communications ✦ Company

Chelsea Clubhouse
1974 Sproul Road, Suite 400
Broomall, PA 19008-0914

The Chelsea House world wide web address is www.chelseahouse.com

Library of Congress Cataloging-in-Publication Data
Ring, Susan.
  Nature did it first / by Susan Ring.
      p. cm. — (Science links)
Includes index.
Summary: Inspiration for invention can come from nature.
  ISBN 0-7910-7427-7
  1. Inventions—Juvenile literature. 2. Inventors—Juvenile literature. 3. Nature—Juvenile literature. [1. Inventions. 2.
Inventors. 3. Nature.] I. Title. II. Series.
  T48 .R56 2003
  609—dc21

                                                          2002015897

Copyright © Newbridge Educational Publishing LLC

Newbridge Discovery Links Guided Reading Program Author: Dr. Brenda Parkes
Content Reviewers: Dr. Sookie Bang, Professor of Biology, South Dakota School of Mines
and Technology, Rapid City, SD; Ronald N. Griffith, Sr. Instructor, Bronx Zoo, Bronx, NY;
James McLurkin, Sr. Research Scientist at iRobot, Somerville, MA; Dr. Anne Moore,
Assistant Professor, Department of Biological Sciences, University of the Pacific, Stockton, CA; Neil Sims, Environmental
Scientist, Oakland, CA.
Written by Susan Ring

Cover Photograph: Dandelion seeds moving gently through the air
Table of Contents: Helicopter in flight

Table of Contents

If the seeds only fell straight down from the flower, the dandelion would not be able to spread its seeds all over.

How Is a Seed Like a Sky Diver?

The tiny seeds of a dandelion spread out far and wide, allowing them to be carried by the wind. The small fluffy tops on each seed gently transport the seeds through the air. In the same way, a sky diver uses a parachute to glide on the wind to a soft landing.

People have always imitated nature. Sometimes an inventor studies an animal or plant to come up with a new tool or method. Other times, even though it is not copied on purpose, we see the same principle at work in nature that we see in an invention. Get ready to discover similarities you never even thought about before!

For hundreds of years, people in Africa have made bridges that look like gigantic spiderwebs. What kinds of materials do you think were used to make this bridge?

Lessons from a Spider

Spiderwebs are spun from silk that a spider makes within its own body. People have copied the structure and design of spiderwebs over and over again. It's not hard to see the beauty in their delicately crafted strands.

Bridges, like spiderwebs, are built using a combination of lines and spaces, creating an interesting and often beautiful design. But besides being beautiful, such designs are able to support a tremendous amount of weight.

This orb weaver uses two kinds of silk: sticky strands that go around in circles and smooth silk for the parts that stick out like spokes on a wheel. The spider walks on the smooth strands, so it never gets caught in its own web!

Incredible Spider Silk

Spiderwebs have fascinating designs, but it's the incredible strength of their silk that people keep trying to understand and imitate.

Spider silk is actually stronger than a strand of steel of the same thickness. It has great tensile strength, which means it can be stretched very far without breaking. Scientists are always looking to create new materials as delicate and light as spider silk and also as superstrong.

What Clues Do Spiders Hold?

What clues could be hidden in a strand of spider silk that might tell us how to make our own materials stronger and better?

Dr. Anne Moore, a biology professor at the University of the Pacific in Stockton, California, is trying to find out. She is examining spider silk under microscopes and other scientific instruments to find out more about its structure.

Black widow spiders, known for their poisonous bite, are her favorite to work with. "Their silk is very strong," she says, "and it's incredibly stretchy." And so far, she hasn't been bitten!

Who knows what will materialize from her studies!

A Sturdy Structure

Some of the most impressive buildings anywhere have not been built by humans. This structure, which towers about 18 feet (5.5 meters) high (that's as tall as a giraffe), is a termite mound. It was built by thousands of termites, each one as small as a pencil eraser.

Termites' engineering skills go beyond those of many other creatures. They make the material to build their mounds by mixing soil with their saliva. The mixture turns into a substance as hard as concrete. And it gets even harder as it bakes in the hot sun. The mound gets so hard that if you tried breaking it with a sledgehammer, you wouldn't even make a dent.

People need to build strong, sturdy structures, too. What do we use to make them?

It takes 10 to 15 years for termites to build a large mound. The walls can be 20 inches (51 centimeters) thick!

Concrete can be molded into many different shapes, as you can see on this building.

Built to Last

Human builders use concrete, which is made from cement, finely crushed stone, and water. It hardens into a very strong material.

But concrete also cracks and it can be costly and difficult to repair it. One scientist is looking for a way to solve this problem.

Dr. Sookie Bang is not a construction worker or an architect. She is a biology professor and a researcher. With funding from the National Science Foundation, she developed a way to repair concrete using the tiniest cement makers. They are a type of bacteria that make their own cement when placed directly  inside the cracks in buildings and statues. The cement combines with the concrete already there and the cracks get sealed.

Her method may be used in the future to repair the cracks in skyscrapers and in historical monuments.

Hummingbirds get their name from the humming sound made by their wings. Helicopters have rotor blades instead of wings.

Fabulous Fliers

Tiny hummingbirds dart into the center of a flower, hover near the petals to sip up the rich nectar, then scoot backward out of the flower and take off. They are the only birds that can fly straight up, straight down, backward, and even hover in midair.

The inventors of the first airplanes watched birds such as gulls, pigeons, and hawks glide on air currents. But the person who designed the modern helicopter wanted to create a different kind of flying machine. He got his best ideas from watching hummingbirds in motion.

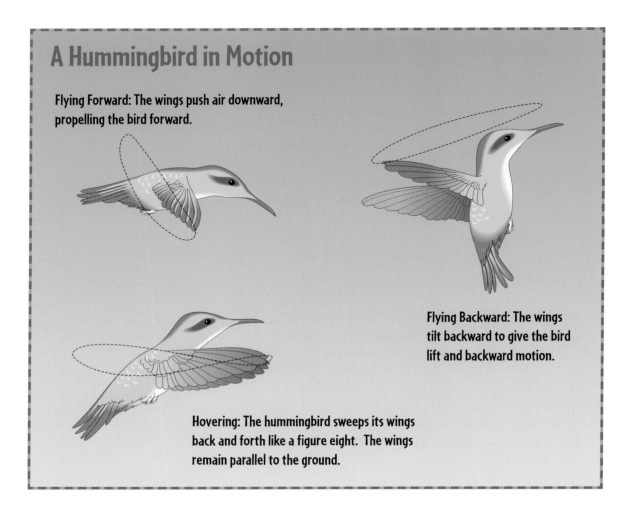

A Hummingbird in Motion

Flying Forward: The wings push air downward, propelling the bird forward.

Flying Backward: The wings tilt backward to give the bird lift and backward motion.

Hovering: The hummingbird sweeps its wings back and forth like a figure eight. The wings remain parallel to the ground.

Small But Powerful

Most birds get power only from the downward movement of their wings. Tiny hummingbirds get power from both upward and downward movement. They beat their wings about 50 times a second, and when making a power dive, hummingbirds can beat their wings about 200 times a second!

An Amazing Flying Machine

Helicopters can do many of the same things a hummingbird can do. Because they can fly straight up and down, they can take off and land without a runway. They can fly backward. They can also hover in midair. For these reasons, helicopters are often used to make rescues and deliveries on top of mountains, buildings, and over water.

When would it be better to use a helicopter rather than an airplane?

An Idea That Stuck

A long time ago, it took a lot of effort for people to get dressed and undressed. They had quite a bit of bending, buckling, buttoning, and lacing to do. But today, you can just zip it, clip it, and rip it with modern inventions.

Velcro® uses tiny hooks and loops to open and close many things. It's used on knee and elbow pads, backpacks, pockets, watchbands, and even medical equipment.

A similar kind of hook–and–loop design is also found in nature. You can see it when you look at a burdock plant.

The larger photo shows what the hooks and loops of Velcro® look like when seen through a microscope. How are the people in the smaller photo using Velcro®?

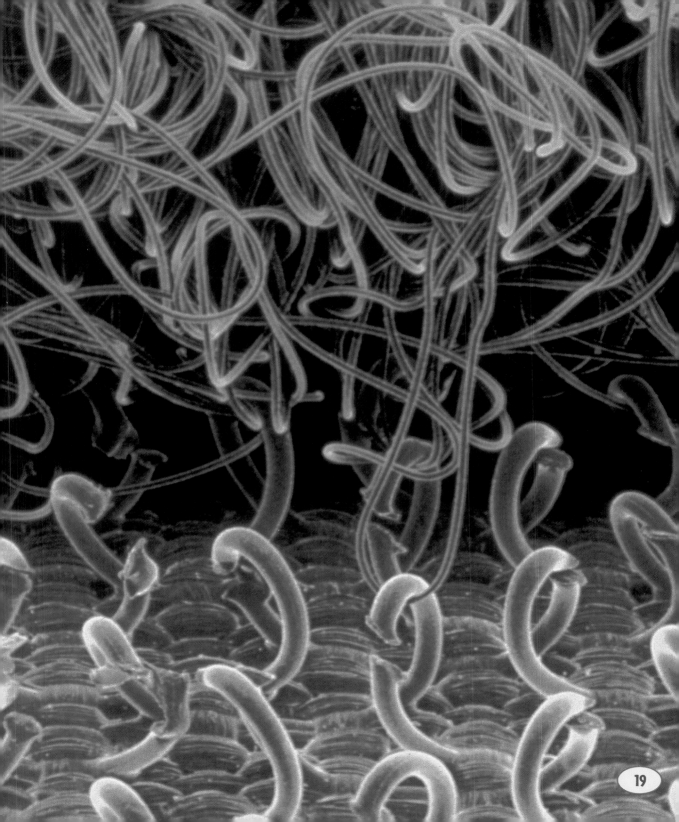

Burdock

Burdock, or goosegrass, is a wild plant. For plants to grow, they must spread their seeds. Some, such as dandelion seeds, blow in the wind. But the burs of the burdock plant do it by grabbing a ride on animals and people. Their little hooks stick to animal fur or people's clothing, and end up wherever they are carried.

That brings us to George de Mestral, the inventor of Velcro®, and what happened after he and his dog took a walk in the woods.

The flowery burs on the tops of the burdock plant are full of tiny hooks.

In 1948, Swiss engineer **George de Mestral** took his usual walk in the woods with his dog. When he got back home, he noticed that they were both covered in prickly burs. He looked at the burs under a microscope and saw that they had hundreds of tiny hooks that grabbed on to the small threads in his clothes and to his dog's shaggy fur. From that, he came up with his idea of using hooks and loops as fasteners. After many years of experimenting, he finally came up with the perfect design . . . a design that stuck.

Why did he call it Velcro®? He used "vel" from the French word *velours*, which means *velvet*, and "cro" from *crochet*, which means *hook*.

Dolphins don't use their mouths to make the clicking sounds used for echolocation. The clicks come from a spot near their blowholes.

Sounds of the Deep

Dolphins' streamlined bodies dive and dart through the ocean. People have always been in awe of their beauty and intelligence. Another amazing thing about dolphins is their ability to navigate under dark water without using their eyes. Instead, they use sound.

Dolphins make a series of clicking noises that bounce off objects. The sound, or echo, that bounces back to them tells them about their surroundings. This is called echolocation. Dolphins' use of echolocation is so focused and exact that they not only know where an object is, but they can determine its size and shape, too.

How do people in submarines use echolocation?

Submarine Sonar

Submarines are built to stay underwater for long periods of time. Like dolphins, they need to "see" what's around them in the murky water. They, too, send out a series of sounds using SONAR (SOund NAvigation Ranging).

A submarine's sonar system sends out sound waves that bounce off objects. The sound returns as an echo to the submarine, where it is then translated into images.

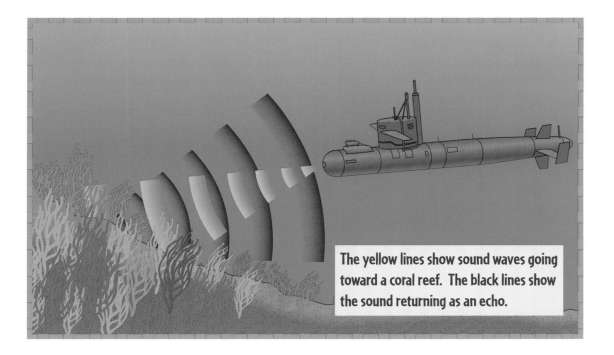

The yellow lines show sound waves going toward a coral reef. The black lines show the sound returning as an echo.

A submarine can dive below the waves or cruise along like other kinds of boats.

This NR-1 submarine used sonar to help scientists make a map of the ocean floor off the coast of Florida. When a submarine sends sound waves to the bottom of the ocean, scientists measure how long it takes for the sounds to return. From these measurements, they can determine the depth and shape of the sea floor. After gathering all their information, they will create a map of the area that shows all the hills, valleys, and coral reefs.

Into the Future

Scientists are building robots to help them study animals. The pike, a fish known for its speed, has been the inspiration for some scientists who want to know more about how fish move.

John Kumph, a scientist in Massachusetts, worked with other scientists to create a robotic pike. The robotic fish swims in a tank and is guided by remote-control radio. By studying the way it moves and turns, he hopes to find out why fish are such powerful swimmers.

Using robotics, scientists can learn about many things seen in nature. Some robots are even put to work.

The robotic pike is weighted so that it swims just below the surface of the water.

Rover the Robot wasn't made to replace sheepdogs, but to imitate their herding behavior.

Rover the Robot

It can't wag its tail or bring your slippers, but Rover the Robot knows how to do its job. Sheepdogs are good at herding other animals. They gather them together and lead them as a group in the same direction. This robot called Rover looks more like a giant tin can than a sheepdog. But it behaves in the same way.

Rover the Robot was developed by a team of scientists. They wanted to find out if ducks would be more comfortable being herded by Rover or by a live sheepdog. What other animals have been copied as robots?

How Do Ants Work?

As a kid, James McLurkin was always playing around with toys and homemade contraptions. Now this scientist has created robotic ants.

His ants are about 1 inch (2.5 centimeters) long and each is powered by its own microcomputer. Their antennae can sense objects that are in their path, which they can decide to pick up or avoid. They are also able to work together hunting for objects or playing tag. What is McLurkin trying to find out?

He wants to know how ants work together as one large group. He is hoping to apply that information to new technology that can help groups of people work together more effectively.

This robot is named Kismet. Its expressions change according to what it "sees."

A Friendly Face

Now there are robots that copy human facial expressions. They are also programmed to respond to certain words and gestures with a smile, a frown, or a look of surprise or anger.

Inventors hope to soon create a robot that could provide help and companionship for a sick person. Such robots might make a phone call, give medicine, or best of all . . . laugh at jokes.

What does the future hold? Who knows? Maybe someday you will come up with the next breakthrough invention. Just remember to pay close attention to nature, because as you've seen in so many cases, nature did it first!

Websites

Invention Dimension:
web.mit.edu/invent/index.html

Innovative Lives:
www.si.edu/lemelson/
centerpieces/ilives/index.html

The Great Idea Finder:
www.ideafinder.com

Index